Acknowledgement of Land & of the Traditional Owners of this Land

I would like to acknowledge the Gadigal people of the Eora Nation, upon whose stolen land I stand on today.
I recognise that this land was never terra nullius — the land belonging to these peoples was never ceded, given up, bought or sold.
I would like to pay my respects to Aboriginal Elders past, present and emerging, and I extend this acknowledgement to all Aboriginal and Torres Strait Islander people.

This book is dedicated to those people that like sex, drugs & rock'n'roll!
-"The Don"

Foreword

Through my window I see Vito.
Who is Vito?
He is a king of Glebe & a good man.
Funny, happy & positive. Lol. Lol.
Every café & restaurant needs a customer like Vito.
We're very happy with Vito.

Roddy
(Owner of The Gardener's Grill)

"The Don" with Roddy

Roddy working at the meat smoker

The Gardner's Grill
Located in the magnificent grounds of Victoria Park, Broadway, Sydney, Australia
thegardenrsgrill.com

Contents

1: It's All in My Head
(E tutta Nella Mia Testa)
2: Emotions
(Emozioni)
3: Let Worlds Collide
(Lascia che i Mondi si Scontrino)
4: 21st Century Woman
(Time of the Matriarchy)
Donna del 21° Secolo (Tempo del Matriarcata)
5: 21st Century Man
(L'uomo del 21° Secolo)
6: It's All a Game
(È Tutto un Gioco)
7: I'm Always Learning
(Mi Imparo Sempre)
8: Why Do I Put People Off?
(Perché Rimprovero le Persone?)
9: Time Heals All Wounds #2
(Il Tempo Guarisce Tutte le Ferite)
10: Doing Nothing is the Hardest Thing to Do
(Non Fare Nulla è la Cosa Più Difficile da Fare)
11: If You Lo❤e Someone, Set Them Free
(Se Ami Qualcuno, Liberala)
12: You Are the Most Boring Person on the Planet
(Sei la Persona Più Noioso del Pianeta)
13: Are you Relevant?
(Sei Rilevante?)
14: The Whale Song
(Il Canto delle Balene)
15: I Tried Everything (To make her fall in LO❤E with me)
Ho Provato di Tutto (Per Farla Cadere in Amore con Me)
16: I Gave My LO❤E Away Too Easily
(Ho Dato Via il Mio Amore Troppo Facilmente)
17: Ageless
(Senza Età)

Contents

18: Say Nothing, Do Nothing
(Non Dire Niente, Non Fare Niente)
19: Attachment
(Allegato)
20: Into the Night
(Nella Notte)
21: I'm Gonna Give Up on Her
(Mi Rinuncia con Lei)
22: She Doesn't Need Me
(Non ha Bisogno di Me)
23: It's Just Talk
(È Solo Parlare)
24: La Vita con Vito
(Life with Vito)
25: Fuck the American Dream
(Fanculo al Sogno Americano)
26: Ignorance is Bliss
(L'ignoranza è Beatitudine)
27: You're Not My Type
(Non Sei il Mio Tipo)
28: The Look of Utter Disgust on Her Face
(Lo Sguardo di Totale Disgusto sul sua Visa)
29: Lo♥e & Lo♥e
(Ama e Lascia che l'amore)
30: Let Go
(Lascia Andare)
31: Won't Get Fooled Again
(Non ti Farai Ingannare di Nuovo)
32: The Universe Has Spoken
(L'universo ha Parlato)
33: She Will Admit to Nothing
(Non Ammetterà Nulla)
34: Hope
(Speranza)

Contents

35: Don't Manipulate Me
(Non Manipolarmi)
36: Rock Poet (Rock'n'Roll Poet)
(Rock Poeta: Poeta Rock'n'Roll)
37: Manifesting, Manifestation
(Manifestazione, Manifestazione)
38: Poetica Politika
39: Welcome to the World of Slavery
(Benvenuto nel Mondo della Schiavitù)
40: My Side of the Story
(Il Mio Lato della Storia)
41: I am An Exhibitionist
(Sono un Esibizionista)
42: An Imperfect Friend
(Un Amico Imperfetto)
43: Stop Making Sense
(Smetti di Dare un Senso)
44: Irreparably Damaged Friendship
(Amicizia Irreparabilmente Danneggiata)
45: The Miguel Treatment
(Il Trattamento Miguel)
46: Ethics verses Morals
(Etica versi Morale)
47: I am Not a Good Friend
(Non Sono un Buon Amico)
48: I Am Delusional
(Sono Delirante)
49: Discombobulated
(Scombussolata)
50: Lo♥e is Not Enough
(L'amore Non è Abbastanza)

It's All in My Head
(E tutta Nella Mia Testa)

It's all a jumble.
It's all a mess.
It's all very crazy.
It's all in my head.

It's all very chaotic.
It's all very problematic.
It's all very confusing.
It's all in my head.

It's all very noisy.
It's all very distracting.
It's all very dramatic.
It's all in my head.

It's all very urgent.
It's all very important.
It's all very "REAL".
It's all in my head.

It's all very disappointing.
It's all very disheartening.
It's all very discombobulating.
It's all in my head.

It's all very lonely.
It's all very sad.
It's all very pathetic.
It's all in my head.

It's all about me.
It's all about my desires.
It's all about my wants.
It's all in my head.

It's all a delusion.
It's all an illusion.
It's all a dream.
It's all in my head.

It's all about LO♥E.
It's all about passion.
It's all about Existence.
It's all in my head.

"The Don"
11.12.2020

Emotions

(Emozioni)

Emotions are so powerful.
Emotions are very strong.
Emotions are very controlling.
Emotions can do you wrong.
Emotions are explosive.
Emotions are destructive.
Emotions are overwhelming.
Emotions are overpowering.
Emotions are chaotic.
Emotions are subversive.
Emotions are coercive.
Emotions are manipulative.
Emotions are consuming.
Emotions are immersive.
Emotions are deceiving.
Emotions are dictatorial.
Emotions are monopolistic.
Emotions are HE♥RT-breaking.
Emotions are Soul-destroying.
Emotions are LO♥E-making.
Emotions are BEAUTIFUL.
Emotions are exhilarating.
Emotions are liberating.
Emotions are unifying.
Emotions are uplifting.
Emotions are Soul-making.
Emotions are HUMAN.
Emotions are LIFE.
Emotions are EXISTENCE.
Emotions are REAL.
Emotions ARE.

"The Don"
11.12.2020

Let Worlds Collide
(Lascia che i Mondi si Scontrino)

Let Worlds collide.
Let's watch them explode.
Let chaos reign supreme.
Let's watch them implode.
Let's watch the fireworks.
Let's watch the show.
Let's sit back & enjoy.
Let's have some fun.
Let it all happen.
Let it all play out.
Let it reach its end.
Let it resolve to its conclusion.
Let yourself be an observer.
Let yourself watch what happens.
Let yourself refrain from interfering.
Let yourself stop from interrupting.
Let yourself be immersed in the show.
Let yourself enjoy the dancing.
Let yourself enjoy the singing.
Let yourself enjoy the romance.
Let yourself enjoy the comedy.
Let yourself enjoy the drama.
Let yourself enjoy the excitement.
Let yourself enjoy the tragedy.
Let yourself enjoy the emotions.
Let yourself cry.
Let yourself laugh.
Let Worlds collide.

"The Don"
14.12.2020

21st Century Woman

(Time of the Matriarchy)
Donna del 21° Secolo (Tempo del Matriarcata)

It's your time to rule.
It's your time to take control.
It's your time to make decisions.
It's your time to play the game.
It's your time to have some FUN.
It's your time to dominate.
It's your time to have the power.
It's your time to experiment.
It's your time to be happy.
It's your time to rule.
It's your time to have the keys.
It's the time of the 21st Century Woman.

You are in control now.
The time of Patriarchy is over.
You are in Power.
The Future is yours.
Do with it what you will.
It's your game now.
It's time to have your fun.
It's time to experiment.
You are your own boss.
You are in charge.
You are in command.
It's the time of the 21st Century Woman.

You don't need men anymore.
You've NEVER needed men.
Men used you.
Men abused you.
Men kept you as a prisoner.
Men kept you as a slave.
Men used you as a sex toy.
Men used you as an object.
Men are now dinosaurs.
Men are now extinct.
It's the time of the 21st Century Woman.

Do whatever you want.
It's the time of the 21st Century Woman.

(This poem is dedicated to Miriam Campana, "The 21st Century Woman")

"The Don"
14.12.2020

21st Century Man

(L'uomo del 21° Secolo)

He's a Neo-Renaissance Man.
He's an Enlightened Man.
In fact, he's not a man at all.
He's a Human Being.
He's the 21st Century Man.

He's gentle.
He's kind.
He's respectful.
He's compassionate.
He's caring.
He's sensitive.
He's LO♥ING.
He's spiritual.
He's the 21st Century Man.

He's an artist.
He's a musician.
He's a poet.
He's a philosopher.
He's a thinker.
He's a carpenter.
He's a LO♥ER.
He's the 21st Century Man.

He's creative.
He's passionate.
He's honest.
He's loyal.
He's witty.
He's Intelligent.
He's truthful.
He's the 21st Century Man.

He's inquisitive.
He's curious.
He's adventurous.
He's funny.
He's serious (when he has to be).
He's emotional (but in a good way).
He's soft (but hard when he has to be).
He's got the goods.
He will deliver.
He's the 21st Century Man.

He's got your back.
He's there to support you (anytime).
He's on call 24/7 (for you).
He won't let you down.
He'll always be there.
He'll be your shelter.
He will LO♥E you forever.
He's the 21st Century Man.

He's tolerant.
He's non-judgemental.
He's understanding.
He's TRUE.
He's the 21st Century Man.

He makes life FUN.
He makes you HAPPY.
He's the 21st Century Man.

"The Don"
15.12.2020

It's All a Game

(È Tutto un Gioco)

Don't take life seriously.
Don't stress out.
Don't panic.
Don't freak out.
Don't be hard on yourself.
It's all a game!

Don't worry.
Don't fret.
Don't get angry.
Don't get sad.
Don't cry.
It's all a game!

Don't be abusive.
Don't be violent.
Don't be cold.
Don't be jealous.
Don't be pathetic.
It's all a game!

Don't wear a frown.
Don't wear a crown of thorns.
Don't be a liar.
Don't be an arsehole.
Don't be a dickhead.
It's all a game!

Don't be a prick.
Don't be a shit hole.
Don't be conventional.
Don't be boring.
Don't waste your life away.
It's all a game!

Don't stay at home.
Don't get married.
Don't take LO♥E too seriously.
Don't fear change.
Don't fear tomorrow.
It's all a game!

"The Don"
16.12.2020

I'm Always Learning
(Mi Imparo Sempre)

I make mistakes.
I fuck things up.
I do the wrong thing.
I say the wrong things.
I piss people off.
I don't mean to.
I have things to learn.

I'm a work in progress.
I'm an unfinished masterpiece.
I'm an incomplete opera.
I'm a symphony that has no composer.
I'm a song without an ending.
I'm a dance with no crescendo.
I'm a painting without a focal point.
I have a lot to learn.

Will I ever be finished?
Will I ever be completed?
Will I ever have my story finished?
Will I ever have my song sung?
Will I ever get to my destination?
I have a long way to go.

There are hurdles along the way.
The road is not always straight.
There are bends & treacherous sections along the way.
There plenty of obstacles along the path.
Keep your eyes always on the path in front of you.
Don't blink.
Don't take your eyes off the road.
You have a long journey in front of you.

There will be distractions along the way.
There will be plenty of disappointments.
There will be many missed opportunities.
There will be many failures.
But don't give up.
Don't be brought down.
You ultimately are strong.
You will prevail.
Because you are always learning.

This is your redeeming feature.
This is your best quality.
This is what will pull you through.
This is your strength.
This will light your path.
This is what will guide you.
I'm always learning.

"The Don"
17.12.2020

Why Do I Put People Off?
(Perché Rimprovero le Persone?)

Can I ask you a question?
Can I get you opinion?
Can you tell me what you think?
Why do I put people off?

Is it something I do?
Is it something I say?
Can you please help me?
Can you tell me what I do wrong?
Why do I put people off?

Am I too loud?
Am I too confrontational?
Am I too obnoxious?
Am I too rude?
Am I too crude?
Why do I put people off?

Are my jokes not funny enough?
Is my laughter too crazy?
Do I say the wrong things?
Do I smell bad?
Am I a prick?
Why do I put people off?

Am I an arsehole?
Am I too old?
Am I a dirty old man?
Am I fucked in the head?
Am I joke?
Why do I put people off?

Don't be shy.
Don't hold back.
Let me have it.
Tell me as it is.
I need to know!
Why do I put people off?

Am I ugly?
Am I stoopid?
Am I an idiota?
Am I disgusting?
Am I repulsive?
Why do I put people off?

"The Don"
17.12.2020

Time Heals All Wounds #2

(Il Tempo Guarisce Tutte le Ferite)

Time heals all wounds.
That's true.
But it takes time.
How much time?
That's the question.
The answer is illusive.
Usually, a lot of time.
But Time heals all wounds.

Time can be deceptive.
Time can be mean.
Time can play with your emotions.
Just when you thought you were healed.
Time reopens the wound.
But let Time do its work.
Don't interfere.
Have faith.
Time will deliver in the end.
It just takes Time.
For Time heals all wounds.

Time has its own agenda.
Time is not beholding to anyone.
Time cannot be rushed.
Time cannot be pushed about.
Time cannot be controlled.
Time cannot be told what to do.
Time is its own master.
Time pulls all the strings.
Time is its own puppet-master.
Time controls its own destiny.
Time is its own boss.
Time controls all.
Eventually, Time heals all wounds.
Eventually.

You are a passenger!
Time is in the driver's seat.
You are a rider astride of Time.
Time decides how fast you'll be travelling.
Time has its foot on the accelerator.
Time will not be rushed.
Time has its hands on the wheel.
Time has its eyes on the road.
Time can go "real" fast.
Time can go "real" slow.
Time won't let you know.
Time is very secretive.
Eventually, Time heals all wounds.
Eventually.

"The Don"
21.12.2020

Doing Nothing is the Hardest Thing to Do

(Non Fare Nulla è la Cosa Più Difficile da Fare)

Don't act.
Don't react.
Don't move.
Don't say a thing.
Don't do a thing.
Don't respond.
Don't make a move.
Don't communicate.
Don't call.
Don't message.
Don't text.
Don't think.
Don't overthink.
Doing nothing is the hardest thing to do.

Stand your ground.
Stand firm.
Stand strong.
Stand still.
Stand robust.
Stand fixed.
Stand stationary.
Stand immobile.
Stand tall.
Stand motionless.
Stand rigid.
Stand emotionless.
Stand stoically.
Stand expressionless.
Doing nothing is the hardest thing to do.

"The Don"
21.12.2020

If You Love Someone, Set Them Free

(Se Ami Qualcuno, Liberala)

If you Love someone, let them go.
If you Love someone, let them be.
If you Love someone, let them be themselves.
If you Love someone, let them do whatever they want.
If you Love someone, give them wings.
If you Love someone, let them fly.
If you Love someone, let them fly away.
If you Love someone, set them free.

If you Love someone, don't tie them down.
If you Love someone, don't chain them to the ground.
If you Love someone, don't clip their wings.
If you Love someone, don't be jealous.
If you Love someone, don't be cruel.
If you Love someone, don't be mean.
If you Love someone, don't control them.
If you Love someone, don't own them.
If you Love someone, don't possess them.
If you Love someone, don't manipulate them.
If you Love someone, set them free.

"Free, free, set them free (Oh whoa)
Free, free, set them free
Free, free, set them free
Free, free, set them free

If you need somebody, call my name
If you want someone, you can do the same
If you want to keep something precious
You got to lock it up and throw away the key
If you want to hold onto your possession
Don't even think about me

If you love somebody
If you love someone
If you love somebody
If you love someone
Set them free."

"If it's a mirror you want
Just look into my eyes
Or a whipping boy
Someone to despise
Or a prisoner in the dark
Tied up in chains you just can't see
Or a beast in a gilded cage
That's all some people ever want to be

You can't control an independent
Heart (Can't hold what you can't keep)
Can't tear the one you love apart (Can't love what you can't keep)
Forever conditioned to believe that we can't live
We can't live here and be happy with less

So many riches
So many souls
Everything we see we want to possess
If you need somebody, call my name
If you want someone

You can do, you can do, you can do the same
If you want to keep something precious
You got to lock it up and throw away the key
If you want to hold onto your possession
Don't even think about me

If you love somebody (Love somebody)
If you love someone (Love somebody)
If you love somebody (Love somebody)
If you love someone

Set them free
Free, free, set them free (Set them free)
Free, free, set them free (Set them free, OW)
Free, free, set them free (Set them free)
Free, free, set them free (Set them free)."

Songwriter: Sting

"The Don"
24.12.2020

You Are the Most Boring Person on the Planet
(Sei la Persona Più Noioso del Pianeta)

You look boring.
You dress boring.
You say boring things.
That's because you have nothing to say.
You have no interests.
You are the most boring person on the planet.

You look beige.
You look insipid.
You have no personality.
You are boring as *"bat-shit"*.
You have nothing interesting to offer.
You are the most boring person on the planet.

You have no interests.
You have no friends.
You get you dates from *"Tinder"*.
You look like a block of wood.
A fish has more personality than you.
You are the most boring person on the planet.

You look like a *"wet"* towel.
You are as riveting as a brown paper bag.
You have no butt.
You are known as *"flat-pack"*.
You live alone.
You are the most boring person on the planet.

You are as romantic as a *"piece of wood"*.
You have the emotions of a *"stone"*.
You are as creative as an ant.
You are as musical as cockatoo.
You have no rhythm & can't dance.
You are the most boring person on the planet.

Although, I might be biased.

"The Don"
24.12.2020

Are you Relevant?

(Sei Rilevante?)

Are you needed?
Are you respected?
Are you required?
Are you sought out?
Are you sought after?
Are you considered?
Are you relevant?

Are you invisible?
Are you dismissed?
Are you ridiculed?
Are you disrespected?
Are you overlooked?
Are you forgotten about?
Are you irrelevant?

Are you curious?
Are you interesting?
Are you informed?
Are you current?
Are you passionate?
Are you creative?
Are you political?
Are you relevant?

Do you still have something to say?

Are you still relevant?

"The Don"
25.12.2020

The Whale Song

(Il Canto delle Balene)

Singing out.
Calling out for its mate.
Where are you?
I need you.

I'm so lonely.
I'm so alone.
I want you.
I'm so alone.
I'm crying for you.
I'm so alone.
I plead for you.
I'm so alone.

Where are you tonight?
The Sun is setting.
The Moon is rising.
Is the Moon *"Full"*?
I hope so.
The *"Full"* Moon is our Moon.
Wherever you are.
Whomever you're with.
When the *"Full"* Moon is risen.
You are with me.
You are mine.
Together we feel each other.

Under the gaze of the *"Full"* Moon.
We are one.
This moment I want to last forever.
But I know it won't last.
I know, in the midst of this ecstatic moment.
I feel extremely sad.
I fee extreme sadness.
Because I know it will END!

I know you will go back to your daily life.
Your boyfriend.
You will forget me until next time.
When the Moon is *"Full"* once again.
The next *"Full"* Moon.

Until then I will be lost.
Shouting out in a sea of longing.
A sea of Desire.
A sea of hoping.
A sea of wishing.
That maybe .....
That maybe .....
You will come back before the next *"Full"* Moon.

The song remains the same.
The tune drifts through the Ether.
Drifts through the Cosmos
Hoping to reach you.
Can you hear its plaintiff cry?
Can you see its tears?
Can you feel it's suffering?
Can you hear its song?

The Whale Song.

"Montage of the Sea"
b/w
Artist:
Vanessa Wells

"The Don"
26.12.2020

I Tried Everything

(To make her fall in LO♥E with me)

Ho Provato di Tutto (Per Farla Cadere in Amore con Me)

I tried everything.
But all I had to do was nothing.
To make her fall in LO♥E with me.

I sang her songs.
I played guitar for her
I sang for her.
I danced for her.
I wrote her poetry.
I tried everything.
But all I had to do was nothing.
To make her fall in LO♥E with me.

I gave her beer.
I gave her joints.
I gave her presents on her birthday.
I gave her presents for Xmas.
I gave her presents randomly.
I tried everything.
But all I had to do was nothing.
To make her fall in LO♥E with me.

I took her to the movies.
I took her to the art gallery.
I took her the beach.
I took her to "Frankie's Pizza".
I took her to the "Van Gogh" exhibition.
I tried everything.
But all I had to do was nothing.
To make her fall in LO♥E with me.

All I had to do was NOTHING.
ABSOLUTELY NOTHING.
But I tried everything.
And all I had to do was nothing.
ABSOLUTELY NOTHING.
To make her fall in LO♥E with me.

"Boy did I FUCK that up!"

"The Don"
27.12.2020

I Gave My LOVE Away Too Easily
(Ho Dato Via il Mio Amore Troppo Facilmente)

I gave my LOVE away too freely.
I gave my LOVE away too cheaply.
I gave my LOVE away too flippantly.
I gave my LOVE away too simply.
I gave my LOVE away too readily.
I gave my LOVE away too casually.
I gave my LOVE away too eagerly.
I gave my LOVEE away too easily.

It got rejected too freely.
It got rejected too cheaply.
It got rejected too flippantly.
It got rejected too simply.
It got rejected too readily.
It got rejected too casually.
It got rejected too eagerly.
It got rejected too easily.

I gave my LOVE away too easily.

"The Don"
28.12.2020

Ageless

(Senza Età)

I have no age.
I have no birth.
I have no Death.
I have no beginning.
I have no end.
I have always existed.
I will always exist.
I am ageless.

My body is just a vessel.
My body is just a container.
It does not define me.
It does not confine me.
It is just where I am.
Where you will find me.
In this moment of *"Astronomical Time"*.
"Astronomical Time" which is measured by the rotation of planets around a Sun.
I also have *"Biological"* time.
Time measured by the breakdown of our cellular structure.
Our body.
I am ageless.

I am measured by neither of these.
For I am outside Time.
I have always existed & I will continue to exist.
I am one of the *"Ancients"*.
Beyond *"Time & Space"*.
Not defined by any moment.
Not defined by any place.
When my biological body can longer function.
I will move on.
I will adopt another form.
I don't know what this form will be.
Or what it will look like.
But one thing I know....
I am ageless.

"The Don"
29.12.2020

Say Nothing, Do Nothing
(Non Dire Niente, Non Fare Niente)

Don't talk.
Don't respond.
Don't act.
Don't think.
Let things unfold before you.
Say nothing, do nothing.

Watch.
Observe.
Look.
Silently.
Refrain.
Say nothing, do nothing.

Let things happen.
Let events occur.
Let the World turn.
Let life take its course.
Let the moment be.
Say nothing, do nothing.

Things will happen.
Without you.
No need to force.
No need to plan.
Events will take place.
Say nothing, do nothing.

This is not Destiny.
This is not Fate.
This is not Fatalism.
This is not Determinism.
This is not "Mechanicity".
Say nothing, do nothing.

This is creating a vacuum.
This is creating a space.
This is creating a void.
This is creating tension.
This is creating polarity.
Say nothing, do nothing.

Something will happen.
Something will fill the vacuum.
Something will occupy the space.
Something will enter the void.
Something will break the tension.
Say nothing, do nothing.

"The Don"
01.01.2021

Attachment

(Allegato)

It's a disease.
It's a sickness.
It's a prison sentence.
It's a "black hole".
It's the "abyss".

It's debilitating.
It's delusional.
It's illusional.
It's confusion.
It's enchainment.
It's containment.
It's incarceration.
It's subjugation.
It's refrainment.
It's imprisonment.
It's destructive.

Fight it.
Reject it.

Do not succumb to it.

It will control you.
It will dominate you.

You will suffer.
You will die.

Do not let it take over.

Attachment is BAD!

"The Don"
06.01.2021

Into the Night
(Nella Notte)

I walk alone.
The deserted streets.
There is no one around.
The darkness is foreboding.
The wind is blowing.
It's starting to rain.
It's a soft patter.
It moistens my face.
I LO♥E the night.
It speaks to me.

It talks about life.
It talks about suffering.
It talks about the He♥rt.
It talks about the Soul.
It talks about LO♥E.
It talks about DEATH.
It talks about loneliness.
It talks about sadness.
It talks about suffering.
It talks about longing.
It talks about lost friends.
It talks about misunderstandings.
It talks about rejection.
It talks about unrequited LO♥E.
It talks about Desires.
It talks about Passion.

The Night is my friend.
The Night is my enemy.
The Night is comforting.
The Night is cruel.
The Night is happiness
The Night is mean.
The Night is a LO♥ER.
The Night is a DESTROYER.

What will the Night bring tonight?
As I walk out.
Into the Night!

"The Don"
06.01.2021

I'm Gonna Give Up on Her
(Mi Rinuncia con Lei)

I'm gonna let her go.
I've had enough.
I've given her my all.
I've given all I've got to give.
But it's just not enough.
So, I'm moving on.
I'm gonna give up on her.

This is my resolution.
I am resolute.
There's no turning back.
I've cut the cord.
I've broken the shackles.
I've cut the chains.
I've become free.
I'm gonna give up on her.

The decision has been made.
The die has been cast.
The burden has been lifted.
I am free at last.
It was hard to do.
Sometimes, I thought I could never do it.
I was bewitched by her
I was entranced by her.
I was enthralled by her.
But not anymore.
I'm gonna give up on her.

I was her captive.
I was her prisoner.
I was her slave.
I was her puppet.
I was her plaything.
Not anymore.
I'm gonna give up on her.

It's all over, baby blue.
'Cause......
I'm gonna give up on her.

And I'm *VERY HAPPY*!

On this day, *EPIPHANY*!

"The Don"
06.01.2021

She Doesn't Need Me

(Non ha Bisogno di Me)

She doesn't want me.
She doesn't care about me.
She doesn't care for me.
She doesn't think about me.
She doesn't LO❤E me.
She doesn't need me.

I'm NOT that important to her.
I'm just a bit of a distraction for her.
She really doesn't care about me that much.
She only comes over when she needs me
She's very hard on me.
She doesn't need me.

She uses me.
She abuses me.
She exploits my good will.
She takes advantage of me.
She takes advantage of my kindness.
She doesn't need me.

But I let her!

"The Don"
06.01.2021

It's Just Talk

(È Solo Parlare)

It's just words.
It's just sounds.
It's just noise.
It's just energy.
It's just frequencies.
It's just talk.

Is it meaningless?
Is it useless?
Is it fruitless?
Is it hopeless?
Is it forgetfulness?
It's just talk.

Hollow words
Hollow sounds.
Hollow noise.
Hollow energy.
Hollow frequencies.
Hollow talk.
It's just talk.

That's all it is.
Don't take it seriously.
Don't make any plans.
Don't buy any tickets.
Don't stock the fridge.
It's just talk.

There's nothing in it.
There's nothing to it.
There's nothing to get excited about.
There's no substance.
There's no reality.
It's just talk.

"The Don"
07.01.2021

La Vita con Vito
(Life with Vito)

La Vita con Vito e come un bicchiere di vino.
La Vita con Vito e come un pate di spaghetti truffolo.
La vita con Vito è come mangiare pasta e fagioli.
La vita con Vito è come mangiare spaghetti arrabbiati.
La vita con Vito è come bere un bicchiere di prosceco.
La vita con Vito è come bere un bicchiere freddo di Peroni Nastro Azuro.
La vita con Vito è come mangiare un salame cacciatora piccante.
La con Vita e la Vita molto bella.

La Vita con Vito e una Vita marviloso.
La Vita con Vito e fabuloso.
La Vita con Vito e interlectuale.
La Vita con Vito e molto sensuale.
La Vita con Vito e super sexuale.
La Vita con Vito e perfecto.
La con Vita e la Vita bella.

La vita con Vito è piena di felicità.
La vita con Vito è tranquilla.
La vita con Vito è gratificante.
La vita con Vito è fantastica.
La vita con Vito è piena di amore
La con Vita e la Vita bella.

"The Don"
07.01.2021

Fuck the American Dream
(Va Fanculo al Sogno Americano)

Fuck America.
Fuck Capitalism.
Fuck materialism.
Fuck money.
Fuck monetarism.
Fuck the Constitution.
Fuck the Republicans.
Fuck the American President.
Fuck Trump.
Fuck nationalism.
Fuck militarism.
Fuck US foreign policy.

Fuck the American Dream.

Fuck the American Dream.

Fuck the American Dream.

Fuck the American Dream.

The American Dream is DEAD!
(if it ever existed)

"The Don"
08.01.2021

Ignorance is Bliss

(L'ignoranza è Beatitudine)

You don't need to know.
You don't need to see.
You don't need to feel.
You don't need to experience.
You don't need to imagine.
You don't need to enquire.
You don't need to find out.
You don't need to access.
You don't need to verify.
You don't need to suffer.
Ignorance is Bliss.

You don't need to be involved.
You don't need to be informed.
You don't need to be a participant.
You don't need to be reported to.
You don't need to be asked permission.
You don't need to be considered.
You don't need to be acknowledged.
You don't need to be a witness.
You don't need to be consensual.
You don't need to be approving.
You don't need to be accessed.
Ignorance is Bliss.

"The Don"
09.01.2021

You're Not My Type
(Non Sei il Mio Tipo)

You're not my style.
You're not COOL enough.
You're not sexy enough.
You're not intellectual enough.
You're not emotional enough.
You're not physical enough.
You're not tall enough.
You're not funny enough.
You're not crazy enough.
You're not smart enough.
You're not cute enough.
You're not fuckable enough.

You're too stylish.
You're too COOL.
You're too sexy.
You're too intellectual.
You're too emotional.
You're too physical.
You're too tall
You're too small.
You're too funny.
You're too crazy.
You're too smart.
You're too cute.
You're too fuckable!

You're just not my type.

"The Don"
13.01.2021

The Look of Utter Disgust on Her Face
(Lo Sguardo di Totale Disgusto sul sua Visa)

The look of utter disgust on your face.
The look of horror.
The look of "*Yuk*"!
The look of "*get out of my face!*".
The look of revulsion.
The look of repulsion.
It was the look of utter disgust on her face.

The look of:
"I've just seen the monster from the Black Lagoon".
"I've just seen the monster from the Swamp Lake".
"I've just seen the most hideous creature that has ever existed".
"I've just seen a monster so grotesquely deformed".
"I've just seen a monster so terrorising it made my blood curdle".
"I've just seen a monster so vile & odious, it sent shivers down my spine".

It was a look I will NEVER forget.
It will be a look that will be etched in my memory FOREVER.
I was shocked by that LOOK.
I freaked out by that LOOK.
I trembled in fear by that LOOK.
It was the look of utter disgust on her face.

It was not the look of Love.
It was not the look of affection.
It was not the look of kindness.
It was not the look of friendship.
It was not the look of caring.
It was the look of utter disgust on her face.

"The monster from the Black Lagoon".
"A hideous creature".
"A strange, deformed, grotesque being".
That's how she SAW me!
It was the look of sheer TERROR on her face.
It was the look of utter DISGUST on her face.

"The Don"
14.01.2021

Love & Let Love

(Ama e Lascia che l'amore)

Live & let live.
Breathe & let breathe.
Sing & let sing.
Dance & let dance.
Roll & let roll.
Flow & let flow.
Free & let free.
Feel & let feel.
Laugh & let laugh.
Fuck & let fuck.
Joy & let joy.
Enjoy & let enjoy.
Hug & let hug.
Touch & let touch.
Smile & let smile.
Cry & let cry.
Hope & let hope.
Dream & let dream.
Love & let Love.

"The Don"
18.01.2021

Let Go

(Lascia Andare)

Let it flow.
Be fluid.
Dispose.
Be loose.
Do not become attached.
Do not form attachments.
Do not possess.
Do not expect.
Do not have expectations.
Just let things flow.
Let things go.

Do not control.
Do not seek ownership.
Let things happen by themselves.
Do not scheme.
Do not manipulate.
Do not plan.
Do not anticipate.
Do not become attached to suffering.
Do not become attached to LO♥E.
Just let things flow.
Let things go.
Let go!

"The Don"
18.01.2021

Won't Get Fooled Again
(Non ti Farai Ingannare di Nuovo)

Too friendly.
Too easy.
Too gullible.
Too weak.
Too pathetic.
Too desperate.
Too blind.
Too attentive.
Too obsessed.
Too obsessive.
Too clingy.
Too needy.
Too open.
Too forward.
Too direct.
Too talkative.
Too transparent.
Too expectant.
Too eager.
Too keen.
Too romantic.
Too LO♥ING.
Too stoopid.
Too foolish.

Too.........
But, I..........
Won't get fooled again!

"The Don"
20.01.2021

The Universe Has Spoken
(L'universo ha Parlato)

The Universe speaks.
The Universe acts.
The Universe is outside us.
The Universe is inside us.
We are one with The Universe.
Listen to its voice.
The Universe has spoken.

The external is within us.
The internal is within us.
We are inexplicably linked.
We are one & the same.
Just like the *"Mobius Loop"*.
What is inside is outside.
What is outside is inside.
The Universe has spoken.

Ever wonder why we do things?
Ever ask yourself self, *"What was that all about?"*
Ever say to yourself, *"What the Hell just happened?"*
Are you ever perplexed by you own actions?
Are you ever perplexed by the actions of others?
Do you ever wonder why things happen the way they do?
Stay calm...
It's just that.....
The Universe has spoken.

Listen to its message.

The Universe has spoken.

"The Don"
27.01.2021

She Will Admit to Nothing

(Non Ammetterà Nulla)

"It's not my fault.
I did nothing.
You humiliated me.
You asked me to leave.
I was just answering him back.
I did nothing wrong".
She will admit to nothing.

I said, *"I was sorry"*.
She said I was an *"arsehole"*.
"Leave me alone!"
"I don't want anything to do with you anymore!"
I could've handled it better.
I accept that.
I could've left the room.
I could've left her alone.
But I did what I did because she was hurting me.
But....
She will admit to nothing.

Maybe, one day she will see things differently.
Maybe, she will put herself in my shoes.
See the situation through my eyes.
Acknowledge that she has to accept some responsibility.
That she was extremely provocative.
That she has a part to play.
And she was not just an innocent bystander.
But, until that day....
If it ever happens.....
She will admit to nothing.

"The Don"
27.01.2021

Hope

(Speranza)

"There is no Hope!"

"What?"
"Are you FUCKING CRAAAAAAAAZZZZZY?"

"There is ALWAYS Hope!"
"Without Hope there is nothing!"

I must live with Hope.
I must have Hope.
I can't help it.
It's the way that I am.
It's in my DNA.
That's the way I'm wired.
I can't do anything about it.

Hope is the word.
It has power.
It has meaning.
It gives LIFE.
It gives LIGHT.
It illuminates the PATH through the Darkness.
It opens the *"Doors of Perception"*.
It allows you to *"walk on through to the other side"*.
It allows you to *"Have the World & to have it NOW!"*

It is NOT *"The END, my friend!"*
It's NOT my *"ONLY friend"*.
It's the BEGINNING.
It's your companion along your journey.
The path can be difficult with many a *"winding road"*.
There will be many obstacles in your way.
But Hope will always be there with you.

If you let it.
If you want it to.
It won't let you down.
It will always be around.
Even in the quietest moments.
Even in the *"Midnight Hour"*.
In the *"Darkest abyss"*.
Hope will be there.
Shining it's LIGHT.

Let there be LIGHT.
Let there be HOPE.
Let there be TOMORROW.

"The Don"
28.01.2021

Don't Manipulate Me

(Non Manipolarmi)

Don't manipulate me with your kindness.
Don't manipulate me with your kind words.
Don't manipulate me with your warm smile.
Don't manipulate me with your warm embrace.
Don't manipulate me with your beautiful music.
Don't manipulate me with your LO♥E.
Please, don't manipulate me!

Don't manipulate me with your soft touch.
Don't manipulate me with your witty repartee.
Don't manipulate me with your humour.
Don't manipulate me with your political views.
Don't manipulate me with your world views.
Don't manipulate me with your LO♥E.
Please, don't manipulate me!

Don't manipulate me with your intelligence.
Don't manipulate me with your poetry.
Don't manipulate me with your guitar.
Don't manipulate me with your singing.
Don't manipulate me with your creativity.
Don't manipulate me with your LO♥E.
Please, don't manipulate me!

Don't manipulate me with your beer.
Don't manipulate me with your gifts.
Don't manipulate me with your apartment.
Don't manipulate me with your dope.
Don't manipulate me with your lighter.
Don't manipulate me with your LO♥E.
Please, don't manipulate me!

Don't manipulate me with your Affection.
Don't manipulate me with your Desire.
Don't manipulate me with your Passion.
Don't manipulate me with your HE♥RT.
Don't manipulate me with your Soul.
Don't manipulate me with your LO♥E.
Please, don't manipulate me!

Don't manipulate me with your generosity.
Don't manipulate me with your sincerity.
Don't manipulate me with your humility.
Don't manipulate me with your Spirituality.
Don't manipulate me with your Humanity.
Don't manipulate me with your LO♥E.
Please, don't manipulate me!

"The Don"
01.02.2021

Rock Poet (Rock'n'Roll Poet)

(Rock Poeta: Poeta Rock'n'Roll)

Wanna be a poet?
Wanna put some words down?
Write down what you think.
Write down what you feel.
Don't hesitate.
Do it!
Be a ROCK poet.
A rock'n'roll poet.

Say it like it is.
Don't sanitise anything.
Speak your mind
Don't hold back.
Don't hesitate.
Do it!
Be a ROCK poet.
A rock'n'roll poet.

Do be embarrassed.
Don't be ashamed.
Don't censor anything.
Just let it flow.
Don't hesitate.
Do it!
Be a ROCK poet.
A rock'n'roll poet.

Let the world know what you think.
Let the world know what you feel.
Don't hold it inside.
You gotta let it out.
Don't hesitate.
Do it!
Be a ROCK poet.
A rock'n'roll poet.

Let the world know what you think.
Let the world know what you feel.
Don't hold it inside.
You gotta let it out.
Don't hesitate.
Do it!
Be a ROCK poet.
A rock'n'roll poet.

Don't give a shit about anyone.
Don't give a FUCK about what others might think.
You don't need their endorsement.
You don't need their VALIDATION.
Don't hesitate.
Do it!
Be a ROCK poet.
A rock'n'roll poet.

Don't worry if you're not "good enough".
Don't worry that it's not "REAL" poetry.
Don't worry about what poetry is supposed to be.
It has meaning for you & that's enough.
Don't hesitate.
Do it!
Be a ROCK poet.
A rock'n'roll poet.

Rock Poet!
I'm a Rock Poet!

Rock Poet!
I'm a Rock Poet!

Sing it!
Rock Poet!
I'm a Rock Poet!

Louder!
Rock Poet!
I'm a Rock Poet!

"The Don"
02.02.2021

Manifesting, Manifestation
(Manifestazione, Manifestazione)

Manifesting.
Manifestation.
Manifesting.
Manifestation.
Manifesting.
Manifestation.
Manifesting.
Manifestation.
Manifesting.
Manifestation.
Manifesting.
Manifestation.
Manifesting.
Manifestation.
Manifesting.
Manifestation.
Manifesting.
Manifestation.
Manifesting.
Manifestation.
Manifesting.
Manifestation.
Manifesting.
Manifestation.
Manifesting.
Manifestation.
Manifesting.
Manifestation.
Manifesting.
Manifestation.
Manifesting.
Manifestation.
Manifesting.
Manifestation.
Manifesting.
Manifestation.
Manifesting.
Manifestation.
Manifesting.
Manifestation.
Manifesting.
Manifestation.
Manifesting.
Manifestation.

"The Don"
02.02.2021

Poetica Politika

The poetry of politics.
The poetry of politicians.
The poetry of power.
The poetry of control.
The poetry of decision-making.
The poetry of governing.
The poetry of government.
The poetry of governance.
The poetry of *"The law Makers"*.
The poetry of leaders.
The poetry of leadership.
The poetry of ruling.
The poetry of rulers.
The poetry of *"People Power"*.
The poetry of *"Power to the People"*.
The poetry of *"The System"*.
The poetry of *"The Establishment"*.

There is no poetry in politics.
There is no poetry in politicians.
There is no poetry in leaders.
There is no poetry in leadership.

Let's put poetry into politics.
Let's put poetry into politicians.
Let's put poetry into leaders.
Let's put poetry into leadership.

I'd like to see a Prime Minister that is a poet!

Has there ever been a President like this?
Yes!
Vaclav Havel, the President of The Czech Republic.
He was a writer & a playwrite.
He started "The Purple Revolution".

Poetry to Power.

The Poetry REVOLUTION!

That is Poetic politics.

That is Poetica Politika.

"The Don"
03.02.2021

Welcome to the World of Slavery

(Benvenuto nel Mondo della Schiavitù)

"Enjoying living in a police state?"
Asked my best friend Stan.
"Yeah!"
"And Lo♥ing it!"

Do you have a permit to be out?
Do you have a permit to enter?
Do you have a permit to sit down?
Do you have a permit to stand here?
Do you have a permit to eat here?
Do you have a permit to laugh?
Do you have a permit to talk?
Do you have a permit to speak?
Do you have a permit to breathe?
Do you have a permit to swim here?
Do you have a permit to live here?
Do you have a permit to hold hands?
Do you have a permit to hug?
Do you have a permit to kiss?
Do you have a permit to FUCK?
Do you have a permit to LO♥E?
Do you have a permit to have children?
Do you have a permit to EXIST?
Do you have a permit to LIVE?
Do you have a permit to DIE?

No?

Then you're FUCKED!

But this is not new.
First nations people have been living like this since colonisation!

Welcome to the world of slavery!

(Inspired from a conversation with "Oka, the Black Queen of Glebe")

"The Don"
03.02.2021

My Side of the Story

(Il Mio Lato della Storia)

I've replayed it in my mind thousands of times.
Over & over.
The events of that fateful night.
What started out as a joke become a nightmare.

You had put yourself back on *"Tinder"*.
You needed to meet more people, you said.
I agreed.
You got two likes straight away.
Maybe it was because of the photo of you in a red bikini.

You were showing me these photos.
We were having a laugh.
It was all a bit of fun.
But then something happened.
It was no longer fun.

You started responding to some dude.
Kissing the phone.
You were flirting with some random guy right in front of me.
It seemed like you were fucking him right then & there.
And I was forced to watch.
I kept looking at you.
I kept looking at your face
This kept on going for quite a while.
I was hoping you would stop.
You didn't.

I start to become agitated.
You seemed to be really getting into it.
I still said nothing.
Still hoping you would stop.
When I realised that you weren't going to stop.
I asked you to stop.
"Stop!"
Don't do this!"
Please, don't do this!"
I repeated this.
She did not stop.

She knew how I felt about her.
I had told her often enough.
That I LO❤ED her.
That she was my *"Soul mate"*.
I knew that she did not feel the same about me.
She told me often enough.
But I guess I'm just a hopeless romantic.
I lived in "hope".
Hoping that one day she would feel the same about me.

It felt like she was plunging a dagger into my HE❤RT.
Twisting it & pushing it deeper & deeper.
Further & further.
Deeper & deeper.

I couldn't breathe.
I was being killed.
I needed to do something.
To protect myself.
To save myself.
It had become a matter of *"self-protection"*.
Otherwise, I would die.
I would be killed.

Was she doing this on purpose?
Was there intent on her part?
Or was she completely unaware of how her actions were affecting me?
I don't know.

I knew what I had to do.
I didn't like it.
I wrestled with myself.
Maybe, I should just do nothing.
Accept it all.
The answer was crystal clear.
There was no hesitation.

"I would like you to leave please!"
"Don't contact me anymore!"
"You are destroying me!"
"It's self-preservation!"
"Have a good life!"

She stood up & said, *"Will you be ok?"*
"I'll be fine", I replied.
She left.

I have since apologised to her.
*"I feel sooooooooo ASHAMED for what I did!
You did not deserve to be treated like that!
I am TRULY sorry!
I hope you can look deep in your HE❤️RT to forgive me!
I do not want to lose your friendship.
As I've told you many times before, you're my soulmate!!!!"*

*"Don't let my stupidity END our FRIENDSHIP!"
"I'm such a FUCKING idiot!"
"I NEVER learn!"
"I wish I could CUT OFF my cock!!!!!"
"That way I would not have any more desires!"
"I am Soooooooooooo SORRY!"
"Let me MAKE IT UP to you!"
"Please forgive me for my STUPIDITY!"*

*"I LO❤️E you sooooooooooooo much!"
"I want to make things right between us."
"We all make mistakes."
"We all regret things that we've done."*

"We all wish we could have done things differently."

I realise now I could & should've reacted differently to that situation.
Left her & gone into another room myself, for example.
But I didn't.

So that is my side of the story, for what it's worth.

"The Don"
04.02.2021

I am An Exhibitionist

(Sono un Esibizionista)

I like to show off.
I like to be funny.
I like to make people laugh.
I like to goof off.
I like to be crazy.
I like to do crazy things.
I am an exhibitionist.

I like to play games.
I like to muck around.
I like to be noticed.
I like to be looked at.
I like to be the centre of attraction.
I like to shock.
I am an exhibitionist.

I like to do crazy things.
I like to be insane.
I like to be mad.
I like to get dirty.
I like to be wild.
I like to take my clothes off.
I am an exhibitionist.

I like that people look at me.
I like that I don't care.
I like to perform.
I like to be a performer.
I like to act out.
I like to be on stage.
I like to be an extrovert.
I like to be on stage.
I am an exhibitionist.

I like to be famous.
I like to be on TV.
I like to be on social media.
I like to be a social whore.
I like to be on Insta.
I like to be on Facebook.
I like to be on Tinder.
I like to be photographed.
I like to be videoed.
.... NAKED.
I am an exhibitionist.

And I LIKE it!

"The Don"
08.02.2021

An Imperfect Friend
(Un Amico Imperfetto)

An Imperfect friend saves you when no one else will.
An Imperfect friend picks you up when you stumble & fall.
An Imperfect friend looks after you & comforts you in your hour of need.
An Imperfect friend takes you to his home when you have nowhere else to go.
An Imperfect friend listens to your story.
An Imperfect friend holds you when you cry.
An Imperfect friend hugs you & tells you that he'll always be there for you.
An Imperfect friend understands your suffering.
An Imperfect friend accepts you for who you are.
An Imperfect friend doesn't want to change you.
An Imperfect friend accepts all your frailties, weaknesses, imperfections, faults & insecurities.
An Imperfect friend sees all the many lives that you've lived in you 42 years on this planet.
An Imperfect friend understands you suffering by being displaced from your beloved Brazil & your family.
An Imperfect friend feels your isolation & your need to travel.... especially to Italy!
An Imperfect friend falls in LO♥E with you.
An Imperfect friend tells you that he's found his *"Soul mate"*.
An Imperfect friend doesn't accept when you say that you will never fuck him.
An Imperfect friend takes tells you that he DOESN'T want to fuck you, he wants to make LO♥E with you.
An Imperfect friend always lives in hope that you will change your mind.
An Imperfect friend will give up everything & travel the world with you.
An Imperfect friend wants to have adventures with you.
An Imperfect friend wants to sing, dance, laugh & do crazy, wild things with you!
An Imperfect friend lets you monopolise YouTube when listening to music.
An Imperfect friend takes you to the beach.
An Imperfect friend takes you to that art gallery.
An Imperfect friend takes you to see the *Van Gogh exhibition*.
An Imperfect friend takes you to *Frankie's Pizza*.
An Imperfect friend lets you sleep over.

An Imperfect friend lets you come over at 4:00am when you call & say *"wake up"*.
An Imperfect friend comes & picks you up from your boyfriend's place at 1:00am after you've had a fight & takes you back to his place.
An Imperfect friend shares his beer & his dope & listens to your story all night long, until the early hours of the morning.
An Imperfect friend sees happiness return you your face.
An Imperfect friend watches over you as you fall asleep on his couch.
An Imperfect friend takes you home the next day.
An Imperfect friend picks you up whenever you call.
An Imperfect friend provides a sanctuary for you.
An Imperfect friend helps you move... twice.
An Imperfect friend lets you be a *"SUPER BITCH"*!
An Imperfect friend takes you to the movies to see Fellini's *"Amacord"* & Nick Cave's *"Idiot Pray"* concert.
An Imperfect friend takes you La Parouse & Nielsen Park.
An Imperfect friend takes you *"Doyle's on the water"*.
An Imperfect friend takes you to see the *"Candlelight Concert Baroque Jazz Fusion"* concert.
An Imperfect friend tells you to leave when you stick a knife into his HE❤RT & look him in his eyes as you plunge it deeper & deeper, twisting it further & further, all the time watching his suffering.
An Imperfect friend pleads for you to please stop, but you do not, you just continue to plunge & twist the knife deeper & deeper.
An Imperfect friend pleads, please don't do this, I'm asking you to stop, but you don't listen you continue, laughing in his face.
An Imperfect friend can no longer take this pain, in an act of desperate self-defence he asks you to leave.
An Imperfect friend doesn't want this, this is the last thing he would ever want, but he has no choice, he must save himself or else he will be destroyed.
An Imperfect friend asks you to please leave.

I could have done things differently, that's true.
I could've done things better, that's for sure.

But that's why......
I'm an *Imperfect friend*.

Are you an *Imperfect friend*?

"The Don"
09.02.2021

Stop Making Sense

(Smetti di Dare un Senso)

Give me some *nonsense*.
Give me some *crazy*.
Give me some *lunacy*.
Give me some *madness*.
Give me some *humour*.
Give me some *fun*.
Give me some *partying*.
Give me some *raging*.
Give me some *anarchy*.
Give me some *idiocy*.
Give me some "*make believe*".
Give me some *fantasy*.
Give me some *imagination*.
Give me some *weirdness*.
Give me some *abstraction*.
Give me some *distraction*.
Give me some *reaction*.
Give me some *fornication*.
Give me some *destabilisation*.
Give me some *revolution*.
Give me some *anti-establishmentarianism*.
Give me some *rebellion*.
Give me some *"Counter Culture"*.
Give me some *"Timothy Leary"*.
Give me some *ACID*.
Give me some *LSD*.
Give me some *Marijuana*.
Give me some *Hash*.
Give me some *Cocaine*.
Give me some *"psychedelia"*.
Give me some *"Flower Power"*.
Give me some *"Flower Children"*.
Give me some *hippies*.
Give me some *music*.
Give me some *Rock'n'Roll*.
Give me some *Beethoven*.
Give me some *Stravinsky*.
Give me some *Dylan*.
Give me some *Hendrix*.
Give me some *pussy*.
Give me some *arse*.
Give me some *LO♥IN'*.

Just....
Stop making sense!

"The Don"
09.02.2021

Irreparably Damaged Friendship
(Amicizia Irreparabilmente Danneggiata)

It is broken.
It is permanently broken.
This friendship cannot be repaired.
There is no use in denying it.
I went too far.
I knew the cost.
I was prepared to pay for it....
...at the time.
Now....
.... I'm not so sure.

Was it worth the price?
Probably not.
Would I do it again.
Probably not.
Would I change what I did if I could go back in time?
Absolutely....YES!

But I really had no choice at the time.
Or so it seemed to me.
I had to protect myself.
I had to defend myself.
I was being attached.
I was being hurt.
I was bleeding.
So, I did what I did.
Knowing full well the consequences of my actions.
I knew that the friendship would be severed forever.
That it could not survive.
I knew this.... at the time.

So, I have no excuses.
I have no defence.
I have no reason to feel rejected by her.
I have blood on my hands!
This I cannot deny.

But, she also, has blood on her hands.
This, she too cannot deny.
Even if she does not want to acknowledge it.
Maybe, one day she will.
Maybe, not.
Who knows what the future will bring?

"The Don"
10.02.2011

The Miguel Treatment

(Il Trattamento Miguel)

He is smooth.
He is handsome.
He loves music.
He does his best work in BED.
He's a man of action.
He never slows down.
He's the best barman in town.
He can make you anything.
From a simple G&T to a fancy, schmancy cocktail.

His laugh is infectious.
His laughter is loud.
His laughter is so loud, you can hear it down the road.
His personality is gregarious.
His hair is long & crazy but he mostly has it tied up.

He will always treat you right.
He always makes you feel good.
He has oodles of charm & wit.
He is also very worldly & wise.
He has travelled to many places.
He has travelled very far, to be here with us.
He is from Bolivia.

He is a musician.
He has an amazing appreciation of all genres of music.
He is very intelligent.
He is very knowledgeable.
He is very curious.
He is very cool.
In fact, he's the COOLEST dude EVER!

Come over sometime to BED Bar in Glebe.
Maybe you'll get to meet him.
Maybe you'll get to see him in action.
Maybe you might get to experience him yourself.
You might even get "The Miguel Treatment".
If you're lucky enough.
Do you feel luck?

Dedicated to my best bro, Miguel!

"The Don"
13.02.2021

Miguel with "The Don"

Ethics verses Morals

(Etica versi Morale)

This has been a continually perplexing dilemma for me.
When is something ethical?
When is something moral?
Are they one & the same thing?
Or are they two distinctly different ideas.

Can you be both ethically & morally correct?
Can you be ethically correct but morally wrong?
Can you be ethically incorrect but morally correct?
Can you be ethically incorrect & morally incorrect?

Is being ethical an issue of *"Right"* & *"Wrong"*?
Is being moral an issue of *"Good"* or *"Bad"*?
What is *"Right" & Wrong"* anyway?
What is *"Good"* or *"Bad"*?
And who defines these?
God?
The State?
An innate human condition?
Spirituality?
The Soul?
Your Heart?
The Universe?
Is it in your DNA?
Your parents?
Society?

To me, it's always been a question of....
.....Ethics verses Morals.

It's all so confusing..........
......so.....I'm just gonna be BAD!

"The Don"
15.02.2021

I am Not a Good Friend

(Non Sono un Buon Amico)

I have been told this many times.
I am not a *"good"* friend.
But I want to be a *"good"* friend.
I want to learn how to be a *"good"* friend.
I want to be a *"good"* friend.

I must learn how to be a *"good"* friend.
I will have to find a teacher.
Someone who can teach me how to be a *"good"* friend.
Someone who can show me what I must do, to be a *"good"* friend.
They will have to take it easy with me.
Because I am a very slow learner.
I have a *"hard head"*.
In Italian, *"testa dura"*.
I am *stubborn*.
I am a *"recalcitrant"*.
But I want to be a *"good"* friend.

I want to be a *"good"* friend so much.
I no longer want to be told that I am not a *"good"* friend.
I want to be the *BEST* friend ever.
Maybe, I should *"Google"* it?
How to be a *"good"* friend?
A quick, step by step guide.
With *"easy to follow"* instructions.
"How to be a "good" friend in 5 easy steps".

Maybe, I should look it up on *"YouTube"*.
It could have a video showing me how it's done.
"How to be a "good" friend made easy!"
"Anyone can do it!"
"Even YOU!"
"YES" this is the one for me.
I can play it back as many times as I want.
Until I get it right.
It would be like learning how to play guitar using tablature.
Without knowing how to read music.
I want to be a *"good"* friend.

I don't want to be told that I'm NOT a *"good"* friend. anymore!
I'm not a *"good"* friend.
I'm not a *"good"* friend.
I'm not a *"good"* friend.
I'm not a *"good"* friend.

"The Don"
16.02.2021

I Am Delusional

(Sono Delirante)

I like to dream a lot.
I live in a fantasy world.
I want to escape from *"Reality"*.
I am delusional.

"Reality" is so dreary.
"Reality" is so boring.
"Reality" is FUCKED!
I am delusional.

I prefer to create my own world.
Prefer to live in a fantasy world.
I prefer to create my own *"Reality"*.
I am delusional.

The *"REAL"* world is full of hatred.
The *"REAL"* world is full of suffering.
The *"REAL"* world is FAKE!
I am delusional.

My *"fantasy"* world is the *"REAL"* world.
My *"fantasy"* world is full of BEAUTY!
My *"fantasy"* world is full of LOVE.
I am delusional.

And I LIKE it!

"The Don"
22.02.2021

Discombobulated

(Scombussolata)

Confused
Disoriented
Unbalanced
Unhinged
Disequilibrated
Uncoordinated
Lost
Mind-blown
Uncentred
Out of sorts
Off kilter
Off the skids
Off the rails.
Off balance
Unbalanced
Unfocused
Spaced out
Blown away
Rattled
Unsettled
Shaken
Unnerved
Unprepared
Not feeling yourself
Disassociated
Disassembled
Unassembled
Distracted
Atomised
Fragmented
Fractured
Shattered
Splattered
Tattered
Torn
Exploded
Imploded
Splintered
Scattered
Fractured
Unaligned
Misaligned
Undisciplined
Unstructured

It's a question of BALANCE.

"The Don"
23.02.2021

Lo♥e is Not Enough

(L'amore Non è Abbastanza)

If you lo♥e someone.
That might not be enough.
They might not feel the same way.
They might not lo♥e you.
The way you lo♥e them.
Sometimes, lo♥ is not enough.

You might find them desirable.
You might find them attractive.
You might fall in lo♥e with them.
You might find them sexually attractive.
You might want to fuck them.
You might want to make lo♥e with them.
But lo♥e is not enough.

They might not find you desirable.
They might not find you attractive.
They might not fall in lo♥e with you.
They might not find you sexually attractive.
They might not want to fuck you.
They might not want to make lo♥e with you.
Lo♥e is not enough.

Sometimes, lo♥e is not enough.
There is no spark.
There is no fire in the belly.
There is no Desire.
There is no passion.
There is no sexual attraction.
Lo♥e is not enough.

Both have to read from the same book.
Both have to be on the same page.
Both have to have the same feelings....
....for each other.
Both have to share the same desires.
Both have to share the same passion.
If not...
...lo♥e is not enough.

Saying "I lo♥e you" means nothing.
Sometimes, lo♥e is not enough.

"The Don"
24.02.2021

"Montage of the Sea"
Artist:
Vanessa Wells

Books written by "The Don"

"My Life with Chickens & other stories: I Pity the Poor Immigrant"
Published:
10th September, 2019
Autobiography Book 1:
0 – 12 years old

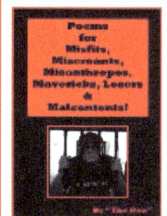

"Poems for Misfits, Miscreants, Misanthropes, Mavericks, Losers & Malcontents!"
Published:
10th June, 2020
Book of Poems 1

"Poems for Troubled Minds & Trouble Hearts"
Published:
10th August, 2020
Book of Poems 2

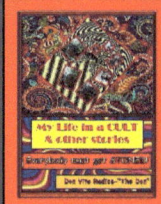

"My Life in a CULT & other stories: Everybody Must Get STONED!"
Published:
10th September, 2020
Autobiography Book 2:
15 – 30 years old

"Poems for Restless Minds & Restless Hearts"
Published:
10th October, 2020
Book of Poems 3

"Poems for Anarchists, Revolutionaries, Outlaws & Dissidents!"
Published:
10th November, 2020
Book of Poems 4

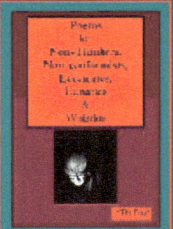

"Poems for Non-Thinkers & Eccentrics"
Published:
10th December, 2020
Book of Poems 5

"The Rantings of a Madman"
Published:
10th January, 2021
Book of Poems 6

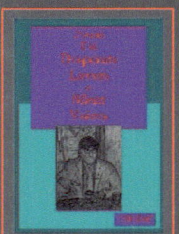

"Poems for Desperate Lovers & Silent Voices"
Published:
10th February, 2021
Book of Poems 7

"Poems for Tormented Minds & Tortured Souls"
Published:
10th March, 2021
Book of Poems 8

All available ONLY online

Books written by "The Don"

"Poems for ALIENS, Outsiders, Outcasts & other STRANGE BEINGS!"
Published: 10th April, 2021
Book of Poems 9

"Poems for Beings From Another Planet"
Published: 10th May, 2021
Book of Poems 10

All available ONLY online

Vito Radice ("The Don"):
Poet/Author/Polemicist/Non-Thinker/Non-Intellectual
To get in touch with "The Don":
Email: donvito7070@gmail.com
Instagram: don_vito_radice
Facebook: Don Vito Radice
Mobile: +61490012461 (Australia)

www.ingramcontent.com/pod-product-compliance
Lightning Source LLC
Chambersburg PA
CBHW041502010526
44107CB00049B/1626